Short ish Walks
Near Exeter

Robert Hesketh

Bossiney Books

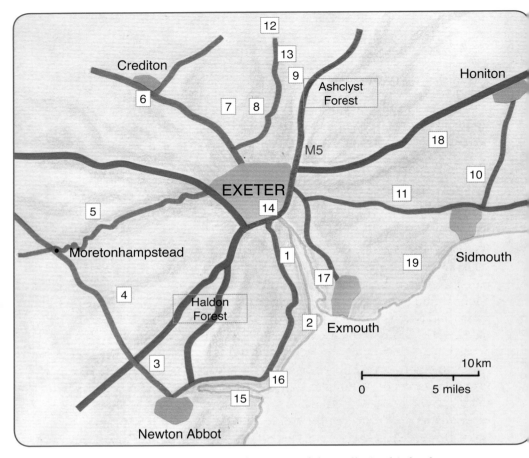

The approximate locations of the walks in this book

First published 2013 by
Bossiney Books Ltd, 33 Queens Drive, Ilkley, LS29 9QW
www.bossineybooks.com

© 2013 Robert Hesketh All rights reserved
ISBN 978-1-906474-40-9

Acknowledgements
The maps are by Graham Hallowell.
Cover based on a design by Heards Design Partnership.
All photographs are by the author.

Printed in Great Britain by R Booth Ltd, Penryn, Cornwall

Introduction

The routes in this book have been chosen to help you explore the beautiful and varied countryside around Exeter. All are within 20 km (13 miles) of the city and most are on regular bus routes. The length of the circular walks varies from 4.3 km up to 9.2 km (2³/₄ to 5³/₄ miles, so the time needed to complete them will vary. Also, some are level, others are a bit more challenging, but why hurry? There are many wonderful viewpoints and places of interest on the way and every walk has its individual character.

Footwear and clothing

Walking is a pleasure throughout the seasons so long as you're prepared. There will be some mud at most times of the year and perhaps a lot of mud and puddles in winter and after rain, especially on the marsh and riverbank walks. Walking boots are ideal, sandals definitely inadequate. Whilst Wellingtons don't breathe or provide ankle support, they are the best option under very wet conditions.

Devon enjoys a mild but changeable maritime climate: it's wise to take extra layers of clothing as well as a waterproof. On some paths there may be gorse or nettles, so trousers are preferable to shorts, especially as they provide some protection against ticks which may carry Lyme disease. If a tick does attach itself to you, remove it promptly and carefully with tweezers.

Extras

Drinking water is a must – you will soon need it and dehydration causes tiredness. I recommend a walking pole or stick too and a mobile phone if you have one. The sketch maps in this book are just that – sketches. You may want to carry an OS Explorer map (numbers 110, 114 and 115 cover the territory) for extra information.

The countryside

Walking is safe and healthy exercise, but please watch out for uneven and waterlogged ground. Despite many pressures on their livelihoods, farmers are still trying to make a living from the land you will pass through. Please respect their crops. Leave gates closed or open as you find them, and keep dogs under control, especially during the lambing and bird nesting season and in nature reserves.

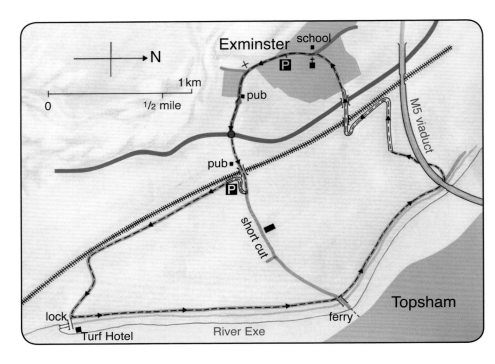

1 Exminster and Exminster Marshes

Distance: 8.4km (5¼ miles) Time: 2½ hours Map: Explorer 110 Character: A largely level route over the RSPB Exminster Marsh reserve and beside the Exeter Ship Canal, with fine views and excellent bird watching, especially in winter. However, parts are prone to flooding after heavy or prolonged rain. Stout boots are recommended at any time.

Start at Exminster's signed free car park near the church. Turn left and follow the main road through the village past the Post Office and the Evangelical Church, where the road bends left. Continue past the Royal Oak to a roundabout on the A379.

Cross carefully and follow the cul de sac ahead, EXMINSTER MARSHES. Cross the railway bridge by the Swan's Nest. Turn right into the RSPB car park. This is an alternative starting point.

Walk to the far end of the car park and take FOOTPATH TO TURF LOCKS on the left. Continue through pairs of gates. Continue ahead, FOOTPATH TO TURF. The path runs parallel to the railway,

then turns left over a footbridge and right over a pair of stiles. Cross the meadow ahead (wet after rain!) to Turf Hotel. The hotel (limited opening in winter) has a lovely beer garden overlooking the Exe – a splendid place to watch waders and wildfowl.

With the canal on your right, turn left up the towpath. Continue to the swing bridge. Here you could turn left (PUBLIC FOOTPATH) as a short cut to the RSPB car park. Alternatively, you could take the foot ferry to Topsham by crossing the swing bridge. Cross the bridge anyway to enjoy the view of Topsham's historic waterfront houses. Alternatively, divert 50 m up the east bank of the canal to the small café.

Recross the swing bridge and turn right, PUBLIC FOOTPATH. Walk upstream with the canal on your right and under the massive M5 viaduct, then turn left over a footbridge and stile. Continue on the path under the viaduct to another footbridge just south of the viaduct, keeping the watercourse on your right.

Cross over a stile and turn right along a track. This bends left and runs parallel to the M5 before bending sharp left to run parallel to the railway. Turn sharp right and cross the railway bridge and the road bridge. Entering Exminster, the track becomes a village lane. This curves left. Turn left opposite the school and follow the main village street back to the car park.

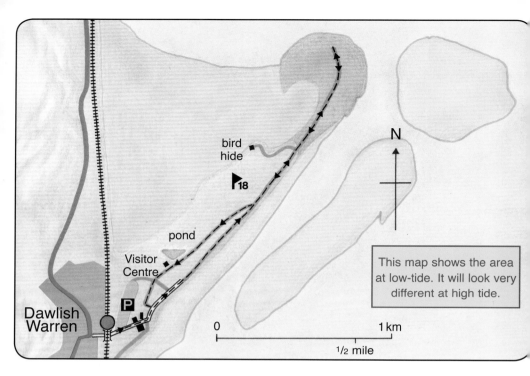

This map shows the area at low-tide. It will look very different at high tide.

bird hide

18

pond

Visitor Centre

Dawlish Warren

P

N

0   1 km
        ½ mile

2 Dawlish Warren

Distance: 5.3km (3¼ miles) Time: 1¾ hours Map: Explorer 110 Character: An easy, level walk with superb coastal views and great birdwatching, especially at high tide and in winter. The Warren is a National Nature Reserve and home to over 600 plant species. NB Dogs are banned from the main beach, but permitted on leads as far as Groyne 9.

Pass under the railway bridge and start your walk from the sea-ward end of the pay and display car park. Follow the tarred path ahead (BEACH) past the toilets and up to the sea wall. Turn left (NATURE RESERVE) and walk past the beach huts along the sea wall with the beach on your right.

When the tarred path ends continue ahead along the sandy path between fences. You may divert down steps to the beach or simply continue ahead parallel to the beach. Continue on the path at a kissing gate, and follow it behind dunes through a second gate.

At Groyne 9 the path runs parallel to the beach again. Keep
to the dune path and avoid disturbing birds by not walking on
the beach three hours either side of high tide or when flocks
are present. Continue on the dune path as it veers slightly away
from the beach and then on until it ends near the tip of the
Warren, with views of Exmouth and the estuary. Retrace your
steps along the dune path.

To visit the bird hide on the north side of the Warren, divert
right down a sandy fenced path. Turn left. Follow the top edge
of the beach, but do not trespass on the golf course and beware
golf balls! After visiting the bird hide, retrace your steps to the
dune path and turn right.

Continue retracing your steps past Groyne 9 and three closely
spaced gates. At the third gate, bear right onto the path through
the Nature Reserve. Follow the path past a bird viewing point
over the marsh and a pond dipping platform to the Visitor
Centre, which has helpful staff and literature, plus displays on
wildlife and geology.

Rejoin the path. When it divides, bear left. At the path junction, turn left and up steps. Turn right at the beach huts and
retrace your steps to the start.

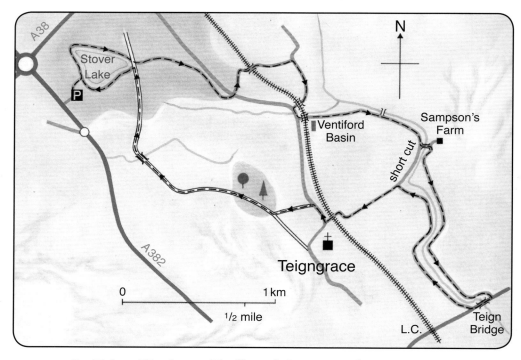

3 Teign Heritage Trail and Stover Lake

Distance: 9.2 km (5³/4 miles) Time 3 hours Map: Explorer 110
Character: A gentle, level walk by lakeside, bankside and
woodland path, this route has abundant wildlife.

Join TEMPLER WAY left of the Visitor Centre and follow it right, down to the shore. Bear left and follow the path around the northern shore of Stover Lake. At the far end turn right across the second bridge and immediately left onto the HERITAGE TRAIL, following it east with the watercourse on your left. Just before reaching the road, turn right as signed. Follow the path through trees and roughly parallel to the road.

Turn right onto the road and almost immediately left, VENTIFORD. Turn right at Ventiford Cottages. Follow the lane beneath the railway bridge. Turn left down the road and left again under Ventiford Bridge. On the right is Ventiford Basin.

Continue ahead as signed to the river bank and bear right downriver. Ignore the first footbridge. At the second footbridge

you could take a short cut by walking on downriver for 200 m and turning right at the waymark post. This reduces the route by 2.3 km (1 1/2 miles). Otherwise, turn left over the footbridge.

Turn left uphill for 100 m to Sampson's Farm café/bistro. This is a substantial thatched building dating from 1480.

Retrace your steps to the footbridge and follow the track for only 70 m. When the track bends right, follow the footpath over the stile as signed. Keep ahead at the footpath junction and follow the bankside path downriver. Turn right onto the road and follow it over Teign Bridge.

Turn immediately right and down steps. Follow the riverbank path for 1.4 km. At the Templer Way waymark, turn left (right if using short cut) and follow the path through fields for 500 m. Turn right and almost immediately left over Locksbridge. Cross the railway carefully to the road by a 16th century farmhouse.

Turn right up the road and left after 150 m. Reaching a quarry, turn right. Stay on the broad track and ignore side turnings. Follow the track through woodland and on over a bridge and into more woodland.

Turn left and follow the southern bank of Stover Lake back to the car park. En route is the aerial birdwatching walkway.

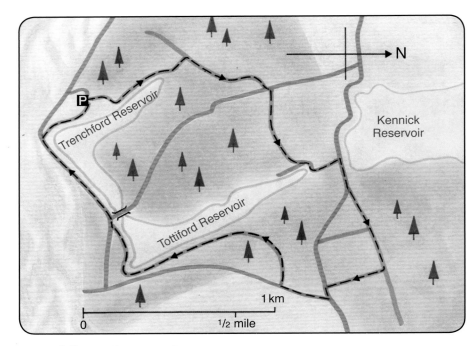

4 Three Reservoirs

Distance: 4.8 km (3 miles) Time: 1 1/2 hours Map: Explorer 110
Character: A gentle walk on the edge of Dartmoor National Park
exploring three linked reservoirs and the mature woodland that
surrounds them.

Start from Bullaton Cross car park and picnic area (SX 804825).
With your back to Trenchford Reservoir turn right, TRENCHFORD
RESERVOIR WALK. The broad path leads past a helpful map of the
reservoirs and on through trees to meet the reservoir bank.

Reaching a signpost at the corner of the reservoir, branch left,
LINKPATH TO COUNTY ROAD. Follow this to a path junction and
turn right, PATH. When the path divides, keep left and uphill.
Stay on the path when it bends left and right.

Cross the lane ahead and take PUBLIC FOOTPATH TOTTIFORD
RESERVOIR. Continue ahead at the path junction to meet the
Tottiford bankside path. Turn left, PUBLIC FOOTPATH TO KENNICK
RESERVOIR. The path turns right at the head of the reservoir, then
left to meet the lane by Kennick Reservoir. Enjoy the view, but

access to Kennick is restricted to fishermen with tickets.

Turn right along the lane, then branch left onto PUBLIC FOOTPATH. Ignore the first turning right. Take the second right, BRIDLEWAY. Meeting the lane, turn left and 100 m ahead turn right, BOVEY TRACEY. Follow the lane for 250 m and turn right, PUBLIC FOOTPATH TOTTIFORD RESERVOIR. Follow the path when it bends left and continue ahead at a path junction, PUBLIC FOOTPATH TOTTIFORD RESERVOIR.

Turn left at the next path junction, TOTTIFORD RESERVOIR PERMISSIVE PATH. This attractive path follows the bank. Continue on the bankside path as it curves right, then left. Meeting a lane, turn right then left at the junction, signed to the reservoir car park. Simply follow the lane beside Trenchford Reservoir to the far corner. Turn right PERMISSIVE PATH TO TRENCHFORD RESERVOIR CAR PARK and follow it to the start.

Of the three reservoirs, Tottiford is the senior. It was constructed in 1861, mainly to supply burgeoning Torbay with water. Demand rose and Kennick, the largest at some 21 ha (50 acres), was built in the 1880s, followed in 1907 by Trenchford.

11

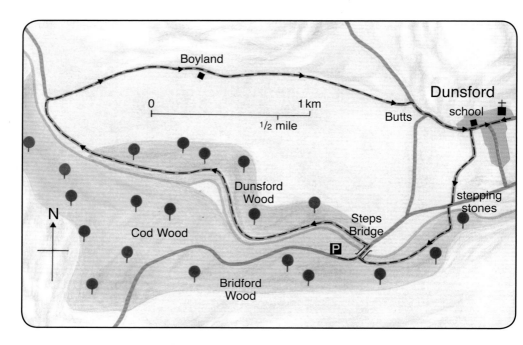

5 Steps Bridge and Dunsford

Distance: 7.3 km (4 1/2 miles) Time: 2 1/2 hours Map: Explorer 110
Character: The first 2.5 km of this route leads along the bank
of the river Teign through Dunsford Woods, a 57 ha (137 acre)
nature reserve famed for its wild daffodils in mid- to late March
– though it's also a great place for woodland birds and deer. The
route is partly level, with one long steady ascent.

Start from Steps Bridge car park, signed off the Dunsford/
Moretonhampstead road. Turn left down the road to cross Steps
Bridge. Turn left, PUBLIC BRIDLEWAY.

Stay with the footpath, which generally follows the riverbank,
whilst the often muddier bridleway diverts inland in places.
Look out for rising trout and salmon, as well as butterflies and
riparian birds such as wagtails, dippers and kingfishers.

Meeting the lane (Boyland Road), turn right. The lane climbs
steadily to 166 m, before descending to Higher Butts Cross.

Carry on ahead, DUNSFORD, taking the pavement as you
approach the village.

Continue to the Royal Oak and divert left to see the church, noted for its fine ceiling bosses and the Fulford memorial. Opposite the church is an array of thatched buildings, including the Post Office and the Walled Garden Tearooms.

Retrace your steps past the village hall and turn left opposite the school, down a short street between thatched buildings to join PUBLIC FOOTPATH B3212. Enclosed at first, the well-beaten path continues across a small field to a line of oaks marked with yellow spots.

Turn left at a field gate. Continue with the hedge on your right. Meeting the road at a metal gate, turn right, then left only 40m ahead, FOOTPATH LEADING TO STEPPING STONES.

Follow the footpath between buildings and over the stepping stones. Follow the path ahead to a junction. Turn right (STEPS BRIDGE) along the tarred track. Branch left at a gate and right at a junction, PATH. Follow the path through woodland above the river to join the road. Turn left to the car park.

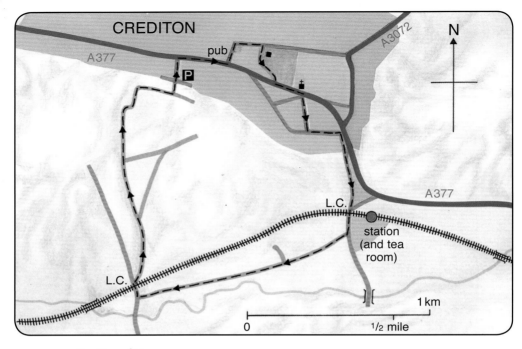

6 Crediton

Distance: 4.9 km (3 miles) Time: 1½ hours Map: Explorer 114 Character: A largely level walk, combining pleasant riverside and field paths with an exploration of Crediton.

You could start this walk from the railway station. If going by car, start from the car park on St Saviour's Way (signed south off High Street). Turn right and downhill to the predominantly Georgian High Street. Turn right along the pavement.

Turn left at the Ship Inn into MARKET STREET and follow it into the Market Square. Cross to the far corner of the Square, bear right and follow the street ahead. Just before the library, turn right down a short path, CREDITON BOWLING CLUB.

Follow the path past the bowling club into Newcombe's Meadow, a public park. Bear left and walk ahead to the St Boniface statue. Follow the path up to the main road. Turn left, then left again at the iron gates to visit Holy Cross Church.

Return to the church gates. Cross the main road and continue ahead into DEAN STREET, one of the oldest in Crediton. Turn left

14

at the junction into Park Street. Walk to the end and turn right into a raised walkway. This diverges right from the main road into FOUR MILLS LANE. Follow this down to the junction. Turn right over the level crossing. Continue past terraced houses.

Turn right, PUBLIC FOOTPATH. When the path divides, fork left through a kissing gate. Follow the path along the right field edge to the riverbank. Continue ahead on the well-beaten path through a kissing gate and parallel to the river through a second gate. Continue on the path with the hedge on your right.

Reaching a lane, turn right past cottages and over a level crossing. Only 40 m ahead, turn right through a gate, PUBLIC FOOTPATH. Follow this path diagonally right uphill to the top field corner. Continue ahead with the field edge on your right.

After 100 m the path divides. Keep left and follow the path through fields with the hedge on your right. Keep left again at the next path junction. Turn right through a gate and up steps along an enclosed path which soon bends sharp left.

Reaching a path junction, turn right along a level tarred path. Turn left and down a path with steep steps. Meeting a T junction of streets, continue ahead and downhill to the car park.

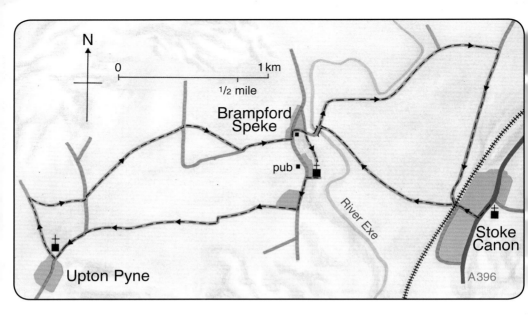

7 Brampford Speke and Upton Pyne

Distance: 5.5km (3¹/₂ miles) Time: 2 hours Map: Explorer 114
This walk can be combined with Walk 8 to make a 10.2km
(6¹/₂ mile) figure of eight route, as shown on the sketch map.
Character: A fairly gentle route exploring a corner of Devon that
inspired pioneering landscape historian WG Hoskins.

Park carefully on Brampford Speke's main street close to the
church. Leave by the south gate. Turn right up the lane and left
along the main village street, or divert right to the Lazy Toad.

At the end of the village, turn right, PUBLIC FOOTPATH. Enclosed
at first, the path enters a field. Continue ahead with the hedge on
your right to a gate. The path again becomes enclosed and then
continues as a well beaten and signed field path. Approaching
Upton Pyne, it becomes an enclosed track again. Continue
uphill to a lane junction.

Turn left and uphill through the village to visit the church.
The tower (1380) has well-restored statues. Inside, there is a
16th century tomb of a warrior in armour, 17th century Flemish
glass and carved capitals. From the church follow the lane uphill
for another 100m. Turn right, PUBLIC FOOTPATH GLEBELANDS FARM.

Follow the track downhill past farm buildings. Cross the stile on the left. Turn right and continue with the hedge on your right to a kissing gate at the end of the field. Here the path divides. Keep right with the hedge on your right to the end of the field. Turn right and continue diagonally right across the field as signed to a kissing gate.

Turn left. Ignore side turnings and continue east to meet a lane. Turn left and after 40 m turn right, PUBLIC FOOTPATH. Follow the enclosed track ahead into a field. Follow the left field edge into a wood and on across another field. Meeting a lane, turn left. After 50 m turn right through a kissing gate. Follow the right field edge and then head diagonally right through the field aiming towards the roofs of houses.

Continue ahead on reaching a lane. At the junction with the main village street, turn left, then right only 30 m ahead past the school. Follow the lane as it curves right behind the school to a kissing gate.

If you wish to join the Stoke Canon walk at this point, turn left and downhill PUBLIC FOOTPATH. Cross the arched bridge and follow directions from point * on page 18. Otherwise, go through the kissing gate and follow the enclosed path to the church.

8   Stoke Canon

Distance: 4.3 km (2 3/4 miles) Time: 1 1/2 hours Map: Explorer 114
This walk may be combined with Walk 7 to make a 10.2 km
(6 1/4 mile) figure of eight route, as shown on the sketch map.
Character: Level walks are scarce in Devon: this gentle route runs
along the bed of the old Exe Valley railway line and over meadows
bordering the Exe. Parts may be wet and muddy after rain.

Park with care on the road near Stoke Canon church. With your back to the church gate, turn left and cross the road. Turn right at the post office into CHESTNUT CRESCENT. Continue over the level crossing. Turn left almost immediately through a gate, PUBLIC FOOTPATH. This joins the bed of the dismantled railway and bends right. Leaving the railway, cross a small footbridge and continue to a much larger arched bridge.

You could join the Brampford Speke walk at this point to make a 10.2 km (6 1/4 mile) figure of eight route. Simply cross the bridge; turn left and follow the path uphill for 170 m. Turn left at the kissing gate and follow the directions from * on page 17.

Otherwise, do not cross the bridge, but follow the concreted

PUBLIC FOOTPATH. When the concrete ends, continue on the grassy footpath. This shortly bends right. Follow the right field edges ahead. The path meets the river. Continue along the riverbank. Cross a stile. The track curves away from the river. When it divides, turn right away from the river along a green lane past Burrow Cottages and Burrow Farm.

Turn right at a stone cross, and follow the tarred lane. Reaching the level crossing, retrace your steps to the start.

WG Hoskins' (1908-92) lifelong fascination with the evolution of the English landscape began on childhood visits to the Exe Valley from his native Exeter. His later researches showed how much of our rural history can be read directly from the enduring marks left by past generations.

Graduating from Exeter University, Hoskins put English landscape studies on the academic map with his *Making of the English Landscape*. He also wrote what is still the standard volume on Devon's history and more than 30 other books, as well as popularising his subject on radio and TV. Professor Hoskins' ashes were scattered at Brampford Speke churchyard.

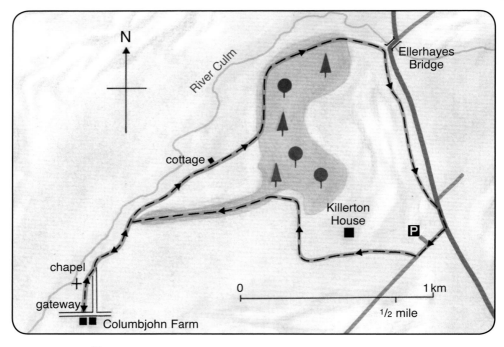

9 Killerton

Distance: 5.7km (3¹/₂ miles) Time: 2 hours Map: Explorer 114
A fairly gentle circuit of the Killerton estate (house and gardens
open through the National Trust) by woodland and field paths.

From Killerton car park (no charge) return to the lane. Turn
right and right again through an iron gate, PUBLIC FOOTPATH.
Follow the grass path parallel to the tarred track. Pass in front
of Killerton House. Continue on the path, which runs parallel to
the ha-ha, a sunken stone wall that separates the lovely gardens
from the surrounding fields and grazing animals, to the hedge
at the end of the field. Go through the kissing gate. Turn right
and uphill, PUBLIC FOOTPATH, keeping the hedge and metal fence
on your right.

   Reaching the top of the slope, do not take the Bluebell Gate
on the right, but turn left along a well beaten grass path to enter
woodland by a gate. Bear left, PUBLIC FOOTPATH. The path divides
almost immediately. Keep left, going through a gate, BEWARE OF
WALKERS. Follow the broad path ahead through Columbjohn

Wood. Reaching a gate at the edge of Columbjohn Wood, walk straight ahead for only 30 m, turn left and follow a broad track, parallel to but at a little distance from the river Culm, for 250 m. Turn right through a kissing gate and follow the fenced path along the right edge of a field past a cottage to see Columbjohn chapel (1851). Divert left down the lime avenue for 180 m to view the old arched gateway, remnant of the 16th century house that preceded the present Killerton House.

Retrace your steps past the chapel and back along the fenced path and broad track to the edge of Columbjohn Wood.

Continue ahead on the broad track to reach a gate with a bridleway sign at the far edge of Columbjohn Wood. Go through this and a second gate. Pass another gate and a cottage. Stay with the track as it re-enters woodland. Continue on the track to the parking area by Ellerhayes Bridge.

Turn right (KILLERTON HOUSE & CHAPEL) and follow the well beaten field path ahead with the lane and field edge on your left. Stay on the path through woodland and small fields, passing a series of gates on the way to meet a lane. Follow the lane past houses, down through a cutting to a junction. Turn right (KILLERTON HOUSE AND GARDEN) and right again into the car park.

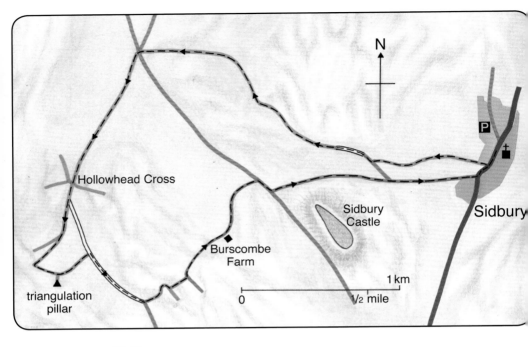

10 Sidbury

*Distance: 8.8km (5¹/₂ miles)   Time: 3 hours Map: Explorer 115
Character: A demanding walk with a long steady climb at the
start and some quite steep descents and one shorter ascent on the
return. Splendid views of woodland and a vista of Lyme Bay.*

Bear right from Sidbury's signed free car park and turn right
into the main village street. Continue for 300m past the Red
Lion and church. Turn right just beyond the telephone booth,
PUBLIC FOOTPATH TO WHITE CROSS. The path climbs steadily past
houses and then along the right edge of a large field. Cross a
stile and continue up the well beaten path. Reaching a lane, turn
right PUBLIC FOOTPATH.

The lane shortly bends left and uphill, becoming a rough
track. Continue ahead at the next gate and follow the path
uphill. The well used path continues uphill through fields and
thence along a line of beeches. Cross the field ahead and leave it
by a metal gate at the top edge.

Turn left to meet a junction almost immediately ahead. Cross the tarred lane and follow the rough track ahead with the pink East Devon Way sign. Continue on this track on a south-westerly course to a junction of paths (Hollowhead Cross). Continue ahead on the East Devon Way. When the track divides, fork right along a beech avenue.

Emerging onto the open heath, fork left along a broad track. This is Fire Beacon Hill Nature Reserve. Turn left, PUBLIC FOOTPATH, at a waymark. Divert right to the triangulation pillar to enjoy the coastal views. Retrace your steps to the main path and turn right. Follow the path when it bends left. Continue through trees to a broad track. Turn right. The track soon becomes stony and descends steeply.

Turn left, PUBLIC FOOTPATH, and follow it through trees to a junction of tracks. Turn right, then shortly afterwards left to follow the path steeply downhill to a gate. Continue steeply downhill through a field to a stile and lane junction. Follow the lane directly ahead, steeply downhill. Walk past farm buildings and Burscombe farmhouse. Follow the lane uphill to a junction.

Turn right. Keep left (SIDBURY) when the lane bends left at a signpost. Follow this lane downhill. Turn left at the junction. Follow the main street back past the church to the car park

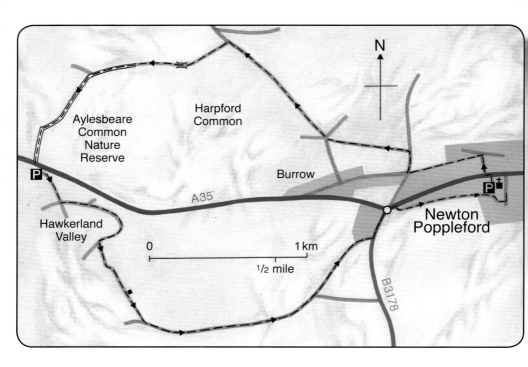

11 Newton Poppleford

Distance: 8.2km (5¼ miles) Time: 2½ hours Map: Explorer 115
Character: A gentle walk over Pebblebed Heaths, with no long or
arduous slopes and much wildlife interest.

Take PUBLIC FOOTPATH TO THE VILLAGE from Newton Poppleford's
free car park behind the church. Walk past the church tower.
Cross the main road carefully. Turn left then almost immediately right down MEADOW DRIVE. Turn left when you reach metal
steps into an enclosed footpath. Continue ahead at a gate.

Reaching a lane, turn right. Take the second lane on the
left. Just before the lane bends sharp left, turn right, PUBLIC
FOOTPATH. Do not take the footpath through the metal gate
on your right, but continue ahead along a broad enclosed
track, PUBLIC FOOTPATH. This leads into the RSPB's Aylesbeare
Common Reserve. Continue ahead along the broad track.

Reaching a tarred lane, continue ahead and turn left, PUBLIC
FOOTPATH. Cross the stream by a footbridge and follow the track

uphill through a metal gate onto a tarred track. Keep on this track, ignoring the footpath on your right. Continue ahead at a crosstracks to meet the main road.

Cross carefully and branch left (HAWKERLAND) across the car park. Attention to the directions and map are needed across the heath of Hawkerland Valley as there are many paths – too many to include them all on the sketch map. Take the path ahead at the signpost and keep right at two path divisions.

Turn left, PUBLIC FOOTPATH, at the crosstracks and waymark. This broad path leads gently downhill with a wood on the left to a junction. Bear half right to join a path through the heath. Keep left when the path divides. Ignore the footpath on your left. Keep on the path as it curves right to the next junction. Turn left here and keep left at the next two path junctions and continue past a cottage.

Reaching a lane, turn left. Follow the lane to a junction. Fork left and follow this lane into the outskirts of Newton Poppleford. Turn left at the T junction and continue to a roundabout. Turn right and almost immediately right again by YE OLDE TOLL HOUSE 1758 into PUBLIC FOOTPATH. This bends left and continues to meet a lane. Turn left and left again into the car park.

12 The Grand Western Canal

A continuous foot/cycle path runs alongside the attractive Grand Western Canal from Tiverton for 18 km (11 1/4 miles), making an easy level walk with good wildlife watching opportunities. Follow the brown road signs to Canal Hill in Tiverton, where there is parking, disabled access, toilets, café and bar and visitor centre.

13 Bickleigh

Following the Exe Valley Way northwards from Bickleigh makes a pleasant and easy stroll by meadows, woods and river bank. There is ample parking by Bickleigh Mill, with its waterwheel and shopping. The walk may be extended to Tiverton, 6 km (3 3/4 miles) each way.

14 Exeter Quay and Canal

Exeter is a wonderful city to explore on foot – *Exeter: A Shortish Guide*, Robert Hesketh (Bossiney Books, 2009) describes five walks around the heart of Exeter and one around Topsham.

Looking upriver to Exeter Quay

Looking north across the Teign on the Shaldon to Ringmore walk

Another attractive and traffic-free 1.5 km (1 mile) circuit starts at Exeter's historic Quay. Follow the Exe downriver from the Quay past the Port Royal, the weir and mill buildings (1730) to Trew's Weir suspension bridge. Cross here and follow the canal towpath back to the Quay.

For a longer walk, follow the towpath south from Trew's Weir to Countess Weir (3.5 km/2 1/4 miles); the Topsham foot ferry (6 km/3 3/4 miles) or Turf Locks and Hotel (7.5 km/4 3/4 miles).

15   Shaldon and Ringmore by the Templer Way

Start from the signed Ness car park in Shaldon. Walk past the Ness Hotel and follow the road ahead past Georgian houses. There is a choice of routes through Shaldon to the bridge. One way is to follow the follow the Strand into the pretty green and thence into Albion Street.

Reaching the bridge, cross the main road. Follow the river-side path – a good place to watch birds. Reaching another road, turn right and continue on the pavement towards Ringmore's Strand. The Templer Way continues along the south bank of the Teign to the Combe Cellars Inn (another 2.5 km/1 1/2 miles) and Newton Abbot. This can only be walked two hours either side of low tide and may be wet or slippery.

16 Teignmouth

Teignmouth's sandy beach and sea front make a splendid, well-surfaced level walk that can be extended for 2 km north of the pier to Holcombe. The town developed as a resort in Georgian and Victorian times. However, it was a port and shipbuilding centre long before that.

For a different view of Teignmouth, follow the sea front south from the pier, round by the lighthouse and on to the Strand with its harbour and waterfront inns and cafes. There is also a ferry to Shaldon. Parking is by the lighthouse and along the sea front.

17 Lympstone

Lympstone is a good starting point for an easy, level walk along part of the Exe Estuary Trail with wide views and good bird-watching, especially at low tide and in winter. Lympstone is 4 km (2 1/2 miles) north of Exmouth on the trail and 2.4 km (1 1/2 miles) south of Exton.

Start from Underhill car park (near The Strand). Turn right and follow UNDERHILL to the Globe Inn. To go south, turn left and follow the lane for 400m, uphill and then down to the river. Turn sharp left for 70m. Turn right (EXMOUTH), where a helpful map board shows the route.

To walk north towards Exton, follow the directions above from the car park to the Globe Inn. Turn right; then turn left at the Post Office. Follow the lane between house backs past the pretty harbour. Keep on the same track as it curves right and uphill to a football pitch. Turn right to join the path by the railway station where there is another map board.

See www.devon.gov.uk/exeestuarytrail for more information.

18 Ottery St Mary

This easy, level route follows a pleasant riverbank path south from Ottery St Mary and may be extended for over 4km/2³/₄ miles to Tipton St John. Cross a footbridge and turn left onto the footpath behind Canaan Way car park. This leads to the unusual tumbling weir. Follow the path behind the derelict factory, the successor to a series of textile and corn mills.

Reaching the road, turn right across the cast iron bridge (1851). Turn left PUBLIC FOOTPATH. Continue past a metal arched footbridge. To avoid marshy ground, the path bears right and slightly away from the riverbank to follow the embankment of

East Budleigh's main street

the disused railway that connected Ottery to Budleigh Salterton.

The path leaves the railway and follows the riverbank more or less closely for the next 2 km.

Just below a large weir, a modern Archimedes screw turbine has been installed on the eastern bank. It generates electricity using water drawn from the river by a leat running from behind the weir. The path continues to a bridge beside an old mill, then onward downriver to meet the dismantled railway just right of its five arched bridge.

On your return, you may wish to explore Ottery St Mary. As well as an attractive medley of historic buildings, it has one of Devon's finest parish churches.

19 Otterton

An attractive and well surfaced path leads south from Otterton alongside the river Otter. Park carefully on Otterton's main street. Cross the bridge by Otterton's working watermill. In various forms it has been in production for over 1000 years and now houses art and craft galleries, shops, bakery and a restaurant/

café. Turn left and downriver. The path may be followed for 3.5 km (2 1/4 miles) to the beach at Budleigh Salterton.

Alternatively, you may wish to divert right after 1.25 km at Clamour Bridge to visit East Budleigh. Keeping the hedge on your right, join the path running along a raised bank. Follow this right and away from the river. Reaching a lane, turn left.

Continue past houses and across the road to the Rolle Arms. Follow the lane ahead into the village. As well as a fine collection of cob and thatched buildings, East Budleigh has a historic church with carved bench ends and Sir Walter Raleigh's portrait. Raleigh is also celebrated at the inn opposite, a character pub with a great collection of period photographs.

Ashclyst Forest

Ashclyst Forest's 300 ha (741 acres) of mixed woodland was planted in the early 19th century. Part of Killerton estate managed by the National Trust, it is crisscrossed by footpaths and

Ashclyst Forest

served by several car parks, the most central being Forest Gate (SX999994). Use the helpful map and information boards to orient yourself or buy a leaflet at Killerton House.

The easiest way to explore is to use the well waymarked walks. Ranging from the disabled path of 800m (1/2 mile) to 5.6km (3 1/2 miles) with a bridlepath of 11.2km (7 miles), these graded routes are designed to show the forest's history, tree species and wildlife. Nationally important for its butterflies, Ashclyst Forest has much more of interest besides, from wild flowers to roe deer and traces of deserted farmsteads.

Each season has its charms: go in spring for flowers, summer for butterflies, autumn for colours and winter to trace the historic remains. Dawn and dusk are the most likely times to spot the shy deer.

Haldon Forest

The Forestry Commission has laid out well waymarked walking trails in Haldon Forest, much of which is coniferous. Designed to be followed without the aid of a map, they are outlined at www.forestry.gov.uk/forestry/INFD-6T7BCW and in free leaflets at Haldon Forest Gateway car park (SX884849), which has several facilities, including café and toilets.

The easiest trails are the all-ability Discovery Trail (2.4km/1 1/2 miles) with fun features for children and the Mamhead Sensory Trails (1.6km/1 mile and 2.4km/1 1/2 mile), both of which are well surfaced. Other trails are themed to help visitors appreciate different aspects of Haldon Forest. They range from the fully surfaced Raptor Trail (5km/3 miles) to the Tree Trail (4km/2 1/2 miles) and the Butterfly Trail (5km/3 miles). All the trails start from Haldon Forest Gateway car park SX884849, apart from the Mamhead Trails, which begin at Mamhead car park SX922807.